Sarah Tyson Rorer

Questions and class Book of the Philadelphia cooking school

Sarah Tyson Rorer

Questions and class Book of the Philadelphia cooking school

ISBN/EAN: 9783744789189

Printed in Europe, USA, Canada, Australia, Japan

Cover: Foto ©Lupo / pixelio.de

More available books at **www.hansebooks.com**

QUESTION

AND

CLASS BOOK

OF THE

PHILADELPHIA COOKING SCHOOL
1525 CHESTNUT STREET

MRS. S. T. RORER
PRINCIPAL

Press of
GEORGE H. BUCHANAN AND COMPANY
420 Library Street 420
Philadelphia

NOTE

When entering upon the practice of my profession, I was greeted with many important questions, relating to the chemistry of food, as well as those pertaining to its special preparations. These ever-recurring questions were "dotted down"—hence this little Class Book.

While I fully realize that the questions herein contained, are not the only ones that might come up in household chemistry lessons, they do cover the most important and useful subjects. Little attempt has been made to classify the questions; one being so nearly related to the other, they form a common whole.

In Class a certain number of questions are given each pupil, who is required, not only to write the answers, but to give a practical demonstration of each.

The Training Classes are under special instructions, and graded diplomas will be awarded pupils passing the examination.

Terms, $10 per quarter of twelve lessons. Materials extra. Private lessons $2 per hour.

Gratuitous lessons will be given to working women, who sign the papers for a three months' course. By this offer we hope to prove that cooking can be made profitable as a trade.

The according of graded diplomas will, we believe, in a few years effect a change of great importance to housekeepers and household help.

S. T. R.

1 What is a range?

2 What is a stove?

3 What is the difference between a range and a stove?

4 Describe the draught of a chimney.

5 Why do new chimneys smoke?

6 What is the difference between a flue and a chimney?

7 What is fuel?

8 What is necessary to kindle a fire?

9 For kindling coal which is the best, hard or soft wood?

10 Explain the difference between hard and soft wood.

11 What takes place after the combustive process has commenced?

12 Is the substance of the fuel destroyed?

13 What becomes of it?

14 Why do soft woods burn more readily than hard woods?

15 What is coal?

16 Describe the different kinds.

17 Which would you use for cooking purposes?

18 Which is best for cooking, large or small coal?

19 Why must we use wood to kindle coal?

20 How should a fire be " fixed " to keep over night?

21 Why does a coal fire remain stationary after it is
   " fixed "?

22 Why must you have an excess of air to kindle a coal
   fire?

23 Is it necessary to use lighter material for kindling wood?

24 Describe coke—charcoal.

25 What fuel produces the largest amount of heat?

26 What is gasoline?

27 Describe a gasoline stove, and tell how to use it.

28 What is coal oil?

29 Describe a coal oil stove, and tell how to use it.

30 What is gas?

31 Describe gas stoves, and tell how to use them.

32 Which is best, and why?

33 Do coke and charcoal require different drafts from other
    fuel?

34 Describe the process of building fires.

35 Describe the different kinds of cooking utensils.

36 What vessels are best to keep their contents warm?

37 Write a list of all necessary utensils in a well-furnished
    kitchen.

38 Name the different kinds of materials used in cooking
    utensils.

39 Which is best, and why?

40 Describe a double boiler, and give its uses.

41 What is the chief objection to iron for kitchen utensils?

42 What are the objections to copper?

43 How can you protect copper utensils—and iron?

44 Is zinc ever used for cooking purposes; if so, why?

45 What might be called perfect cooking utensils?

46 What is the composition of these utensils?

47 What may be said of the glazing on earthen vessels?

48 Describe the method of cleaning these various utensils.

49 How are alimentary principles divided?

50 What are simple aliments?

51 What are compound aliments?

52 What are the non-nitrogenous—and what the nitrogenous?

53 What other element have we which belongs to neither?

54 What is one of the most important properties of water?

55 What is this combination called?

56 What is a saturated solution ?

57 Has water the power to dissolve all substances ?

58 Does it act alike on all substances ?

59 Which dissolves a solid substance more readily, hot or cold water ?

60 How must you proceed to dissolve salt and sugar quickly ? Why ?

61 Is there any perfectly pure natural water ?

62 Which of the natural waters is the least contaminated ?

63 Why is boiled water flat to the taste ?

64 How can you tell the difference between hard and soft water?

65 For cooking green vegetables, would you use hard or soft water? For dry vegetables?

66 If hard water was not at hand, how would you proceed to make it—and soft?

67 For cooking meats would you use hard or soft water?

68 Can meat always be cooked in water?

69 Is the temperature of boiling water always the same? If not, why?

70 What occurs in boiling?

71 Of what do these bubbles consist?

72 Where are the bubbles formed?

73 Do they rise to the top of the water?

74 What becomes of them?

75 What happens after the heat continues long enough for these bubbles to rise to the surface and escape into the air?

76 What influence has the air pressure upon boiling? Why?

77 Does the weight of the liquid itself affect its boiling?

78 Does salt water boil at a higher or lower temperature?

79 Is water boiling violently hotter than that which boils moderately?

80 Does water boil if dropped on a highly heated metallic surface? Why? Give an example?

81 Does milk or water boil (bubble) in a double boiler?

82 What is the difference between boiling and baking?

83 Are things more wholesome boiled or baked?

84 How is starch affected by boiling?

85 What would you do with tough meat?

86 Give the chemical composition of meat.

87 How is it affected by boiling?

88 What is the difference between boiling and simmering?

89 Can meat be thoroughly cooked at a lower temperature than boiling-point?

90 Give the proper methods for cooking meat in water.

91 What is simmering-point?

92 What is the difference between baking and roasting?

93 Give the best method of baking meats.

94 Describe the oven dampers and their proper positions while baking.

95 Which is more highly flavored, roasted or baked meat? Why?

96 With what should meat be basted?

97 Give the proper method of roasting and broiling meats, and the difference.

98 Give the proper method of roasting and baking poultry and game.

99 What is rare meat? Under-done? Well-done?

100 What is the proper temperature for roasting or baking?

101 Should the temperature be stationary throughout the entire cooking; if so, why?

102 What is braising? Describe the proper method.

103 What kind of meats are better braised?

104 What is frying?

105 What is the proper temperature for frying?

106 Are fried articles wholesome? Why not?

107 What material is best and most wholesome for frying purposes?

108 Which heats more quickly, vegetable or animal oil?

109 Give the method for frying in vegetable oil. In animal oil.

110 Do you fry in boiling fat?

111 What do fats contain when bubbles appear on the surface during the heating process?

112 What causes the spattering and boiling as articles are immersed?

113 Must we have separate supplies of fat to fry fish, croquettes, etc.?

114 What utensils are necessary for frying?

115 What is cooking in a small quantity of fat called?

116 Which is more palatable or wholesome, this or frying?

117 How do you clarify fat?

118 What precautions should be taken while frying in fat?

119 If a small quantity of fat is spilled and takes fire, what is the best way of removing it?

18

120 What sort of fat is best for frying doughnuts and fritters? Why?

121 What is the most economical way of cooking meats?

122 By which process is the greater loss in weight? Why?

123 How great is that loss?

124 What is beef? Mutton? Veal? Lamb? Pork?

125 Tell how beef is divided.

126 What constitutes good beef?

127 What pieces are best for roasting or baking? Broiling? Stewing? Frying?

128 What piece would you select for mince meat? Soup?
Beef tea?

129 Tell how mutton and lamb are divided.

130 What constitutes good mutton or lamb?

131 What pieces are best for roasting or baking? Broiling?
Stewing? Frying?

132 What piece would you use for mutton broth?

133 Tell how veal is divided and what constitutes good veal.

134 What pieces are best for roasting or baking? Stewing?
Frying?

135 Tell how pork is divided and what constitutes good pork.

136   What pieces are best for roasting or baking?   Frying?

137   What parts would be used for sausage?   Lard?   Bacon?
        Larding pork?   Flitch?   Scrapple or puddings?

138   What is souse?

139   What internal organs of animals are used for food?

140   Describe each and tell from what part of the animal
        it is taken.

141   Give the proper methods of cooking each.

142   What is tripe?   What is said of its digestibility?

143   Which is the more easily digested, beef or mutton?
        Why?

144   Which is the more nutritious?   Why?

145   What is said of the digestibility of pork and veal?

146   What is fibrin?

147   What is the difference between the juices and blood of meat?

148   What is the difference between suet and fat?

149   What is the thickening principle of soup?

150   What is gelatin?

151   Why does veal or lamb broth coagulate sooner in cooling, than that of beef or mutton?

152 Would you use hot or cold water to make soup? Why?

153 When should salt be added to meats in cooking? Why?

154 What gives odor and flavor to meats?

155 To what class of foods do meats belong?

156 What is said of the digestibility of warmed-over meats?

157 Which is the most wholesome way of serving them?

158 Are the heads of animals ever used for food?

159 What is haggis?

160 What is corn beef? What is dried beef? Give the best methods of cooking.

161 Give the classification of vegetables. Give examples.

162 To what family does the potato belong? What condiment belongs to the same family?

163 Give the chemical composition of potatoes.

164 How are they affected by heat?

165 Which is the more healthful, baked or boiled potatoes?

166 Why do old potatoes wilt after sprouting?

167 Which are the more nutritious, old or new potatoes? Why?

168   What is the nutritious principle of potatoes ?

169   Why are potatoes heavy and sodden if not boiled?

170   Is the juice of potatoes acid or alkaline ?

171   Give the proper methods for cooking potatoes.

172   In boiling potatoes should you use hard or soft water ?
      Why ?

173   Why are fried potatoes indigestible ?

174   What are Jerusalem artichokes ?

175   Describe the methods of cooking them.

176   Describe the chemical composition of beets; turnips; carrots; parsnips; salsify; horse-radish.

177   Give the proper methods of cooking each.

178   Do vegetables contain albumen and casein?

179   What is the difference between vegetable and animal albumen and casein?

180   Give the names of all vegetables containing casein.

181   Give the chemical composition of the onion.

182   Give the different varieties of onions, and the best methods of cooking each.

183   What are leeks? Chives? Garlic?

184 Give the difference between a Spanish and an American onion.

185 How do you get onion juice?

186 Of what vegetables do we eat the leaves?

187 Give the chemical composition of each and the best methods of preparing them.

188 What is the difference between water-cress and pepper-grass?

189 Of what vegetables do we eat the stalks?

190 Give the chemical composition of each and the best methods of preparing them.

191 What is asparagus?

192   Give its chemical composition and the best methods of
       preparing it.

193   Of what vegetables do we eat the flowers?

194   Give the best methods of preparing each.

195   Of what vegetables do we eat the fruit?

196   Give their chemical composition and the best methods
       of preparing each.

197   What is sauerkraut?

198   What are chick peas?

199   What are lentils?

200 What are Brussels sprouts?

201 What is kohl-rabi?

202 What are mushrooms? Truffles? Morels? How can you distinguish the poisonous from the edible ones?

203 What vegetable is more capable of sustaining life, weight for weight, than any other kind of food?

204 Of what vegetables do we eat the seeds?

205 Give the chemical composition of each and the best methods of preparing them.

206 From what is oil produced?

207 Is there any difference between vegetable and animal oil? If so, what is it?

208 What is the difference between oil and fat?

209 What is the difference between a fixed and a volatile oil?

210 What vegetables produce the most oil?

211 What animals produce the most oil?

212 How do oils differ from other alimentary principles?

213 Do oils produce muscle or heat?

214 What is said of the digestibility of oil?

215 What vegetables contain volatile oils?

216 Name the cereals.

217 Describe the wheat grain. Give its chemical composition and the processes of making it into flour.

218 How may the quality of flour be determined?

219 What is the indigestible portion of the wheat grain? Why?

220 What articles of food are made from the glutenous part of wheat?

221 How does heat affect the starch cells of wheat?

222 What causes the variations in flour?

223 Why is fine flour white and whole flour dark?

224 How does age affect flour ?

225 What is farina ?

226 Give the best method of making white bread; bran bread.

227 What constitutes the perfect loaf?

228 Beside good flour and water, or milk, what other element is necessary for bread ?

229 What is yeast?

230 Give the proper method of making yeast, and keeping it.

231 Why do you use potatoes for yeast ?

232 To increase the growth of yeast, must you scald or freeze it? If so, why?

233 Can any other ferments be used in making bread? If so, describe them.

234 Give a recipe for salt-rising bread.

235 What is leaven?

236 Why does bread made with leaven have an acid flavor?

237 Which is the best and most healthy ferment for daily bread?

238 In what temperature should the sponge be kept?

239 Why must it be thoroughly beaten?

240 About what amount of liquid will moisten four quarts of flour?

241 What may be added to flour to make it hold more water?

242 Why is dough elastic?

243 Why do we knead bread? Describe the whole process.

244 Why are the hands the best instruments for this purpose?

245 How do you know when to cease kneading?

246 What makes the dough rise?

247 What is moulding?

248 How can you tell when bread is ready for baking?

249 At what temperature should the oven be?

250 How can the oven be tested without a thermometer?

251 How long should bread be baked?

252 What is the difference between the crust and the crumb, and what causes the difference?

253 Why is the crust sweeter than the crumb?

254 How can you determine when the bread is done?

255 Why should bread be exposed to the air after it is removed from the baking-pans?

256 How should bread be cared for after it becomes cold?

257 Why does fermentation take place more quickly in bran bread than white?

258 What is rye? Describe the grain, and give its chemical composition.

259 How may its nutritive quality be compared with that of wheat?

260 Give the proper method of making rye bread.

261 Why is the method so entirely different from that of wheat bread?

262 What is corn? Name the different kinds, and give their chemical composition.

263 Give best methods of preparing green corn.

264　Why will corn-meal not make loaf bread?

265　What is samp? Hominy?

266　How are they prepared?

267　Why does corn-meal spoil quickly?

268　What is the difference between white and yellow ~corn-meal?

269　Give recipe and example for a good corn bread.

270　What is mush? Give recipe for making it.

271　Describe the oats grain, and give its chemical composition.

272 How does it compare in point of nutritive value with other grains ?

273 Give recipe for oat-meal mush, with example.

274 What is groats ?

275 Describe the rice grain, and give its chemical composition.

276 What is said of its digestibility ?

277 What is the proper method of boiling it ?

278 What is barley ?   Pearl barley ?

279 For what is pearl barley generally used ?

280 Describe the buckwheat grain, and give its chemical composition.

281 Give the proper method for making buckwheat cakes.

282 What are fruits?

283 What fruits are most commonly used as articles of diet?

284 What is said of the nutrition of fruits?

285 Why are fruits useful as foods?

286 Which is the most important of our native fruits?

287 Are apples important as regular diet?

288 Are fruits usually cooked or eaten raw ?

289 What are compotes ?

290 Give recipe for making apple sauce from fresh apples ; from dried apples.

291 What is the best method of stewing prunes ?   Dried peaches ?

292 How do you bake apples ?

293 Give method, with example, for fruit dumplings.

294 What is vegetable jelly or pectin ?

295 What is fruit jam ?

296 Why do fruit jellies, if boiled too long, lose their gelatinous properties?

297 What is the difference between evaporated and dried fruits?

298 With what are fruit jellies usually adulterated?

299 Give the chemical composition of milk.

300 What is said of its nutrition and digestibility?

301 What is the fatty matter of milk?

302 Which is the most nutritious, skimmed or whole milk?

303 At what temperature does milk boil?

304   What is the acid of milk?

305   What is sugar of milk?

306   What is the difference between raw and boiled milk?

307   What is casein?

308   What forms the thin skin covering boiled milk?

309   Is it necessary for milk to boil for cooking purposes?

310   Which is more healthful, sweet or sour milk?

311   What is koumiss, and how is it made?

312 What is said of its digestibility?

313 Give full directions for making butter.

314 Why does it become rancid?

315 How do you clarify butter?

316 What is oleomargarine? Butterine?

317 How may you determine the difference between false and true butter?

318 What is bonny clabber?

319 What is schmier-käse?

320 How is it prepared ?

321 What is cheese ?

322 What may be said of its nutrition and digestibility ?

323 When should uncooked cheese be eaten ?

324 Which is more easily digested, cooked or uncooked cheese ?

325 Give four popular methods of cooking cheese, with examples of each.

326 What is the chemical composition of eggs ?

327 What may be said of their nutrition and digestibility ?

328 At what temperature does the albumen coagulate?

329 Give the proper method for soft-boiling an egg.

330 Which cooks more quickly, the yolk or white?

331 How may you determine fresh eggs without breaking them?

332 Why does a good egg sometimes "rattle"?

333 Which is the most nutritious, the yolk or white?

334 How is the nutrition of eggs compared to that of beef?

335 What kind of eggs are usually employed for cooking purposes?

336 Why do eggs become lighter as they grow older?

337 How may eggs be preserved during the winter season?

338 Give the most wholesome ways of cooking eggs.

339 What is the proper method of poaching an egg?

340 Give the names of fish in common use.

341 Give the chemical composition of fish.

342 What is said of its nutrition?

343 At what season are fish best for food?

344 How may you determine a fresh fish?

345 What fish are best for boiling? Broiling? Frying? Baking? Planking?

346 Give the proper method for boiling, frying, baking and broiling fish.

347 Do fish contain albumen?

348 How is the nutrition of fish compared to that of beef?

349 What causes the flesh of some fish to be white, and that of others colored?

350 Give the proper method of washing fish.

351 What effect does the moon have upon fish? Why?

352 What fish are best to salt?

353 What is the best method of freshening salt fish?

354 Give the best method of cooking, with example.

355 Give three methods of cooking salt cod.

356 What are eels? How should they be cleaned and cooked?

357 What fish have no scales?

358 What is the edible part of frogs?

359 Give the best methods of preparing frogs.

360 What fish have the oil distributed throughout the body?

361 What are sardines? Give the best method of cooking them.

362 Name the shell-fish in common use.

363 Are shell-fish as nutritious and digestible as fish?

364 Which is the most easily digested of the shell-fish?

365 What part of the oyster should be rejected as indigestible?

366 Describe the stomach and liver of the oyster.

367 What proportion of the oyster is liver?

368 At what season of the year are oysters not eatable?
Why?

369 Give the popular methods of preparing, with example.

370 Give the proper method for boiling and opening a
lobster.

371 Should lobster be dead or alive before boiling?

372 When would you use male and when female lobsters?

373 In buying boiled lobsters, how may you determine
whether or not they were alive immediately before
boiling?

374 What is the coral of lobster?

375 When are lobsters in season?

376 What is a "tom ally"?

377 What is the "lady" of the lobster?

378 Give recipes, with examples, for common methods of preparing lobster.

379 What are crabs? . Give methods of boiling and opening.

380 Give recipes of most common ways of preparing them.

381 What are soft-shell crabs, and how are they cooked?

382 What is the "apron"?

383 What are craw-fish?

384 What are prawns?

385 What is the usual manner of preparing them?

386 What are shrimps? What two kinds are usually sold
     in our markets?

387 What may be said of canned shrimps?

388 Give the method of boiling and opening shrimps.

389 Give the best methods of preparing shrimps.

390 What are scallops? How are they sold? What part
     is used for food?

391 Give the best methods of cooking.

392 What are mussels or soft clams ?

393 At what season are they used ? Give the proper methods
     of opening and cooking.

394 What are clams ?

395 What three varieties are in common use ?

396 When are they in season ?

397 What may be said of their digestibility ?

398 Which variety is best ?

399 Give the proper method of opening, and the best
     methods of cooking them.

400 What are terrapins?

401 How are they sold, and when are they in season?

402 What is the difference between diamond backs and other varieties?

403 What are red-legs?

404 Give the method of boiling and opening a terrapin, and the best method of cooking.

405 How would you select a chicken? Turkey? Duck?

406 How can you tell the difference between a young and an old turkey? Duck? Chicken?

407 Give the proper method of cleaning and trussing poultry and game.

408 What are the giblets? How are they cleaned?

409 Give recipe for roasting and boiling a chicken.

410 What is a brown fricassee? White fricassee?

411 Give recipe for broiling a chicken.

412 What are capons?

413 What is the best method of cooking them?

414 What is a galantine of turkey?

415 What is a salmi of duck?

416   How can you distinguish a young from an old goose ?

417   What are guinea fowls, and how are they best cooked ?

418   What is venison ?

419   What is said of its nutrition and digestibility ?

420   Give three common methods of preparing it.

421   Give the proper method of cleaning rabbits or hares,
      and the best methods of cooking them.

422   How may the fishy taste be removed from a wild duck ?

423   What varieties are considered best, and how may they
      be distinguished ?

424 Name the birds in common use for cooking.

425 Describe each, and give its best methods of cooking.

426 Name the nuts in common use. Tell how and where they grow.

427 What is said of their nutrition and digestibility.

428 What nuts are used for cooking purposes?

429 What is tea? Give its chemical composition and active principle.

430 Describe its growth. Name and describe each of the different species.

431 Which is more healthful, green or black tea? Why?

432 Show an example of the tea nearest perfect.

433 Why should tea always be made in an earthen vessel ?

434 Why should it not be boiled ?

435 Name the different kinds of coffee, and describe each species.

436 Tell where and how it grows.

437 Give its chemical composition and active principle.

438 Give the best methods of making coffee.

439 Why should it not be boiled?   Are coffee and tea infusions or decoctions?   Why ?

440 Which is the more healthful, tea or coffee?

441 What is chicory, and its uses? How do chicory and coffee differ in chemical composition?

442 What is cocoa? Tell where and how it grows.

443 What is chocolate? Broma? Racahout? Alkathrepta?

444 Give their chemical composition.

445 What is the active principle of cocoa?

446 What is the best method of preparing each?

447 What is tapioca? Arrow-root? Sago?

448 To what class of food do they belong?

449 Name the different kinds of arrow-root. Which is best?

450 Why called arrow-root?

451 What is corn-starch? What are its uses?

452 How many tablespoonfuls of pure corn-starch will thicken a pint of milk for puddings?

453 Give recipe for blanc mange. Chocolate pudding.

454 What is Irish moss? Iceland moss?

455 Give the chemical composition and their uses.

456 What is sugar? Give adulterations.

457 How can you tell grape from cane-sugar?

458 What is maple-sugar?

459 What is caramel?

460 Name the different kinds of sugar and tell their uses.

461 How do you clarify sugar?

462 What is honey? Syrup? Molasses?

463 What kinds of molasses are best for cooking purposes?

464 Is sugar a preserver?

465 What is the best method of determining the density of sugar? Give example of boiling.

466 Can candy be made from uncooked sugar?

467 What is salt? What is its chemical composition?

468 What are condiments?

469 How many kinds of pepper are used?

470 What is white pepper? Black? Cayenne? Bird?

471 What are pepper-corns?

472   To what family does cayenne belong ?

473   Which are best, male or female nutmegs ?

474   What are nutmegs ?   Tell where and how they grow.

475   Why are nutmegs limed before exporting ?

476   What is mace ?

477   What is curry powder ?   Give recipe for making.

478   What are coriander seeds ?   Cumin seeds ?   Fennel
      seeds ?   Anise seeds ?

479   What is turmeric ?

480 What are cloves? Describe the structure of the clove.

481 What is allspice? By what other name is it known?

482 What gives the grains their shriveled appearance?

483 What is cinnamon? How is it prepared?

484 Where is it principally cultivated?

485 What other spice is usually mixed with it before exportation?

486 What is ginger? Where and how does it grow?

487 What is Jamaica ginger?

488   What are its principal uses ?

489   What are mustard seeds ?

490   What is the difference between brown and white mustard ?

491   What is mustard flour, and what are its principal uses ?

492   What are hops ?   For what are they used ?

MISCELLANEOUS

What is the difference between isinglass and gelatin?

What is glycerin?

What is potato starch?   Flour?

What is oat flour?

How many tablespoonfuls of flour will thicken a pint of milk for sauce?

How do you make French salad dressing?

What is mayonnaise?

How do you pull candy?

How do you thaw meat or poultry?

How do you use a salamander?

What is gumbo fillet powder?

What is vanilla, and for what is it used?

How do you make vanilla sugar?

How do you make a jelly bag?

What is a pastry bag?   What are its uses?

How do you whip cream?

How do you glacé fruits?

What is the best method for cleaning currants?

Why does boiling water poured over dry gelatin toughen it?

What are orange baskets, and how are they made?

How do you blanch and salt almonds?

What is larding? How is it done? What meats are best larded?

What are lardoons?

Describe a larding needle and a trussing needle.

Why is lard better for greasing cake pans than butter?

Should you measure flour before or after sifting?

What is baking-powder?

Give a formula for baking-powder made from tartaric acid. Another from cream tartar.

If you put a cold article in an oven, while a cake is baking, what will happen to the cake?

How should you look at a cake while it is baking?

How can you tell when a cake is done?

Do cakes containing butter require a moderate or hot oven? Cakes without butter?

How should you turn a cake from the pan when done, and where should you place it to cool?

Give recipe and example for cake without eggs.

What are cookies? Apees?

What are buns? Rusks?

How do eggs produce lightness?

What produces the lightness in pastry?

Why must starch be cooked?

What changes are produced in fat by heat?

What may be said of the digestibility of pastry and puddings?

What is a pot pie?

Describe a perfect kitchen.

What food should be kept in a refrigerator?   A cellar?
A dry closet?   Dark?   Light?

Why do foods spoil?

What kind of refrigerator is best?

What kind of diet is best for brain workers?

What would be the consequence of an exclusive meat diet?

Why does it take a polished surface longer to heat than a rough one?

Name all the vegetable acids, and tell in what vegetables they may be found.

What flesh contains most fibrin?

What is glue?

What are leguminous seeds?

Why cannot you make bread from bean meal?

Why does a steel knife blacken in cutting apples?

Why do fruits decay quickly ?

How do ripe and unripe fruits differ in chemical composition ?

What so-called " *weeds* " are edible ?

What is asparagin ?   What vegetables contain it ?

What gives flesh its red color ?

What causes dough to sour ?   Can this sourness be removed ?

Why cannot you use yeast with molasses ?

What is dextrin ?

What is rennet?   How does it thicken milk ?

What is whey ?

What is clotted cream ?

How does salt act in preserving meats ?

What effect does it have upon the fibrin ?

What happens to vegetables soaked in salt water ?

What flesh contains phosphorus ?

What kind of soup is most strengthening ?

Why are cakes less digestible than bread?

What is vinegar, and from what is it produced?

What is starvation?

Why is ice water injurious?

What are supposed to be brain nutriments?

Why should breakfast be eaten soon after rising?

Why are late suppers injurious?

What are liquid foods? Solid foods? Semi-solid foods?

Of what use are acids as aliments?

Why do you use an acid in mayonnaise?

What is the "mother" in vinegar?

What is cacao butter?

Why does cream come to the surface of the milk?

What is the greatest quantity of oil that can be worked
into the yolk of one egg?

How can mayonnaise be "brought back"?

How do albumen and oil differ in composition?

How do you wash meat and jelly bags?

What is the general principle of cleansing?

What is the difference in texture between woolen, cotton and linen fabrics?

How would you remove oil stains from wood?

What is cookery?

Write six menus for breakfast, dinner and supper, of simple, wholesome and nutritious food, with meat and without.

Plain Course

First Lesson

Soup Stock
Baked Rib of Beef with York-
    shire Pudding
Mashed Potatoes

Cottage Pudding with Lemon
    Sauce
Lima Beans

Second

Tomato Soup
Meat Croquettes
Broiled Steak, Tomato Sauce

Ribbon Potato
Custard Soufflé

.

Third

Potato Soup
Stew of Beef with Dumplings
Cold Slaw
Macaroni à l' Italienne

Boiled Rice
Sponge Cake
Tea

Fourth

Pea Soup
Boiled Leg of Mutton, Caper
    Sauce
Potato Salad

Carrots
Corn
Beauregard Eggs
Apple Dumplings

Fifth

Purée of Carrots
Chinese Mutton
Scallop of Mutton
Curry of Mutton

Mutton on Toast, Tomato Sauce
Spinach, Egg Dressing
Gingerbread

Sixth

Plain Paste
Chicken Pie
Apple Pie

Chocolate Pie
Oyster Pie
Patties

Seventh

Bread
Parker House Rolls
Cinnamon Buns

Soda Biscuit
Muffins
Coffee

Eighth

Vegetable Soup without Meat
Veal Cutlets
Hominy
Beets

Parsnips
Baked Potatoes
Batter Pudding with Foam
Sauce

Ninth

Fish Soup
Deviled Fish
Boiled Haddock
Cusk à la Crême

Mackerel, à la Maitre d'Hotel
Sauce
Fish Balls
Tapioca Cream

Tenth

Oyster Soup
Fried Oysters
Panned Oysters
Scalloped Oysters

Broiled Oysters
Oyster Croquettes
Oysters à la Béchamel

Eleventh

Mock Bisque Soup
Plain Omelet
Lamb Chops
Broiled Ham

Rice Griddle Cakes
Frizzled Beef
Victoria Corn Cakes

Twelfth

Pepper Pot
Roast Chicken, Giblet Sauce
Toad in Hole

Potatoes, Hashed
Eggs Fondu
Cheese Straws

Advanced Course

First Lesson

Mock Turtle Soup
Fricassee of Chicken
Pilaff of Chicken

Boiled Rice
Orange Cream
Berwick Sponge Cake

Second

Soup à la Reine
Chicken Croquettes
Chocolate Cake

Lyonnaise Potatoes
Charlotte Russe

Third

Black Bean Soup
Fillet of Beef with Mushroom
Sauce

Scalloped Tomatoes
Delmonico Potatoes
Angel Cake

Fourth

Fish Chowder
Baked Haddock, Sauce Hollandaise
Fish Salad

Salmon Croquettes
Smelts
Cream Meringue

Fifth

Cream of Celery Soup
Sweetbread Croquettes
Sweetbreads, Béchamel Sauce

Potato Croquettes
Pound Cake
Bavarian Cream

Sixth

Turkish Soup
Casserole of Chicken
Chicken Salad

Cheese Ramakins
Iced Rice Pudding with Compote of Fruit

Seventh

Oyster Loaf
Oyster Stew
Oyster Cream
Oysters in Oil
Fricassee of Oysters

Panned Oysters
Little Pigs in Blankets
Broiled Oysters
Hamburg Cream

Eighth

Puff Paste
Oyster Patties
Richmond Maids of Honor
Rissoles

Lemon Custard
Marlboro Pies
Pineapple Pie

.

Ninth

Boiled Lobster
Deviled Lobster
Lobster Chops

Lobster Salad
Wigwam Pudding
Sunshine Cake

Tenth

Potted Pigeons
Fricandeau of Veal
Chicken Fillets

Grafton Cake
Orange Sherbet

Eleventh

Boned Turkey
Montrose Pudding

Salted Almonds

Twelfth

Braised Leg of Mutton
Hamburg Steaks
Strawberry Charlotte

Omelet Soufflé
Spice Cake

Fancy Course

First Lesson

Birds in Potato Cases
Baked Mushrooms
Veal Olives

Coffee Cake
Fruit Croquettes

Second

Bouillon
Soufflé of Chicken
Timbale of Chicken

General Satisfaction
Queen Mab's Pudding

Third

Consommé
Partridges on Toast
Macaroni Croquettes

Potted Chicken
Tutti Frutti

Fourth

Puff Paste
Vol-au-Vent of Oysters

Mirlitons
Pigeon Pie

Fifth

Truffled Turkey Stuffed with
Chestnuts

Chaud Froid of Chicken with
Aspic Jelly
Charlotte Russe

Sixth

Beef à la Mode
Game Pie

Iced Cake with a Compote of
Gages
Café au Lait

Seventh

Squabs and Peas
Terrapin

Stuffed Eggs
Baked Ice Cream

Eighth

Fillet of Beef, Mushroom Sauce
Scallops

White Mountain Cake
Café Noir

Ninth

Baked Salmon, Sauce Hollandaise
Rolled Steak

Broiled Lobster
Frozen Apricots

,

Tenth

Ragout of Wild Duck
Calf's Head
Sweetbread Cutlets

Chicken Fillets
Bird's Nest Eggs

Eleventh

Suprême of Chicken
Fondu of Parmesan
Krapfen

Chocolate Éclairs
Chocolate

Twelfth

Beef Grenadines
Asparagus in Ambush

Orange Baskets
Nesselrode Pudding

Pastry Course

First Lesson

Plain Paste
Lemon Pie
Lemon Custard

Peach Meringue
Rissoles

Second

Puff Paste
Patties
Richmond Maids of Honor

Raised Pie
Strawberry Meringue

Third

Apple Jelly
Preserved Pineapple

Calf's Foot Jelly
Fruit Cake

Fourth

English Plum Pudding
Pound Cake

Bisque Ice Cream

Fifth

Alaska Bake
Strawberry Soufflé

White Mountain Cake
Café Parfait

Sixth

Apees
Jumbles

Cream Puffs
Frozen Apricots

Seventh

My Queen Pudding
Lady Cake

Cocoanut Drops
Baba Pudding

Eighth

French Fruit Pudding
Angels' Food
Montrose Pudding

Cheese Straws
Cheese Fingers

Ninth

Orange Marmalade
Orange Soufflé, Frozen

Biscuits Glacé
Dominoes

Tenth

Orange Cake, Vanilla Sauce
Sherbet

Café Frappé
Fruit Glacé

Eleventh

Macedoine of Fruit
Shaddock Sherbet

Ice Cream Cake
Kisses

Twelfth

Bombe Glacé
Jumbles

Charlotte Russe
Strawberry Bavarian Cream

www.ingramcontent.com/pod-product-compliance
Lightning Source LLC
Chambersburg PA
CBHW021416090426
42742CB00009B/1163